KITTENS

Sandie Lee Books

Kittens

You have probably seen a kitten or you may have even had one as a pet. Kittens make great companions. They are super fun to play with and to watch, but like all baby animals, the kitten has special needs. In this article we are going to explore all the things about kittens. We will discover what they eat, how they learn and some specific breeds. Let's get started on our journey through the world of kittens.

Newborn Kittens

Did you know there is around 80 different breeds of kittens? Kittens can be born any time of the year, but spring and summer are mostly when it happens. Newborn kittens are born blind, deaf and helpless, with very little fur. Kittens depend on their moms for everything at this stage of their lives.

What Kittens Eat

Did you know kittens nurse milk from their mother? Mother cat can feed a litter of kittens all at the same time. Each kitten is supplied milk from the mother's teat. The milk is full of nutrients to help her kittens grow. The kittens knead their mother with their tiny paws to make the milk flow.

How Long With Mom?

Did you know kittens can leave their mother as young as 5 weeks old? Although kittens can survive on their own this young, it is best if they stay with mom a little longer. Most kittens should be allowed to stay with their mother until they are at least 8 weeks of age.

Kitten Talk

Did you know kittens can communicate? Newborn kittens will use a long drawn-out squeal when they feel lost or lonely. Short squeals mean, "I am hungry." As the kitten gets older, it will be able to meow. And of course, all kittens purr. However, purring can mean your kitten is happy, sad or even in pain.

Getting Teeth

Did you know a newborn kitten's teeth are so tiny you can't see them? A kitten's teeth start to show at about 4 weeks of age. With such tiny teeth, the kitten will only be able to drink milk from its mother. At around 4 weeks-old, the kitten will try to sample other food.

Sleeping Kitten

Did you know kittens sleep about 18 hours a day? Like all babies, kittens sleep to conserve energy, restore their bodies and to grow. As the kitten ages, it will spend less time sleeping. But even adult cats like to take 'cat naps' and so will a kitten. These quick sleeps last about 30 minutes.

Playing Kitten

Did you know kittens learn a lot through playing? When a kitten is very young it will crawl along the floor on its belly. But once it gets its legs up, watch out, because the kitten will start to run everywhere and chase everything. Kittens will also tumble and play with their siblings. This is fun to watch.

Learning to Meow

Did you know some kittens can have around 16 different meows? Kittens are very vocal right from birth. But as they age, their meows will change. You may notice a different voice for wanting food, being petted, or even to just be left alone. Siamese kittens are known for their loud voices and different meows.

Learning to Hunt

Did you know kittens are born knowing how to hunt? This is called, instinct. But even though deep down inside they want to hunt, they still have to learn. Kittens learn to hunt by chasing toys, creeping up on their littermates and by pouncing. Kittens will practice hunting all the time they are playing.

Learning to Bathe

Did you know kittens like to bathe themselves? Newborn kittens are bathed by their mother. She uses shortlicks with her tongue. As the kitten gets older, it will watch and learn from its mother how to bathe. By 4 weeks of age, the kitten is usually trying to clean all his/her parts.

Learning About the Litter

Did you know kittens are quick to learn how to use a litterbox? When kittens are newborn, mom will lick their underside to make them go to the bathroom. Once the kitten is older and moving about they can use a litterbox. Kittens have an instinct about covering up their waste and they learn very quickly.

The Bengal

The bengal kitten is a cross between an Asian Leopard cat and a domestic cat. These kittens tend to be bigger than average kittens. They have a beautiful coat that can be silver, brown, snow or blue. They also have remarkable patterns that can be striped or spotted in black. Some can even look like miniature leopards.

The Scottish Fold

The Scottish fold kitten is very unique in appearance. Instead of ears that stand straight up, this kitten has ears that are folded downward and forward. To look at this kitten it would appear it doesn't have any ears at all. This breed originated from a barn cat named, Susie, in Scotland.

The Sphynx

The Sphynx kitten is perhaps the oddest of them all. It is born hairless and stays that way! This kitten have huge ears, wrinkly skin and patterns on its skin where fur would be if it had any. The sphynx kitten will grow up to be a larger cat and, of course, needs to be kept warm.

Quiz

Question 1: A newborn kitten is very helpless. What are the other things about a newborn kitten?

Answer 1: It is blind, deaf and has little fur

Question 2: How many hours a day do newborn kittens sleep?

Answer 2: About 18 hours each day

Question 3: Some kittens are very vocal. How many different sounds can they make?

Answer 3: Some breeds can make up 18 different calls

Question 4: How do kittens learn to hunt?

Answer 4: Playing, pouncing on toys and with their littermates

Question 5: Which breed of kitten has folded ears?

Answer 5: The Scottish fold

Thank you for checking out another addition from Sandie Lee Books! Make sure to check out Amazon.com for many other great titles.

www.ingramcontent.com/pod-product-compliance
Lightning Source LLC
Chambersburg PA
CBHW040328010626
45792CB00024B/2286